What is a plant?

Louise and Richard Spilsbury

www.heinemann.co.uk/library
Visit our website to find out more information about Heinemann Library books.

To order:
 Phone 44 (0) 1865 888066
 Send a fax to 44 (0) 1865 314091
 Visit the Heinemann Bookshop at www.heinemann.co.uk/library to browse our catalogue and order online.

First published in Great Britain by Heinemann Library, Halley Court, Jordan Hill, Oxford
OX2 8EJ, part of Harcourt Education.
Heinemann is a registered trademark of Harcourt Education Ltd.

Editorial: Kate Bellamy
Design: Jo Hinton-Malivoire and AMR
Illustration: Art Construction
Picture Research: Ruth Blair and Kay Altwegg
Production: Severine Ribierre

Originated by Repro Multi Warna
Printed and bound in China by South China Printing Company

The paper used to print this book comes from sustainable resources

ISBN 0 431 01803 0
ISBN 978 0 431 01803 4
10 09 08 07
10 9 8 7 6 5 4 3 2

British Library Cataloguing in Publication Data
Splisbury, Louise and Richard
What is a plant? – (World of plants)
581

A full catalogue record for this book is available from the British Library.

Acknowledgements
The Publishers would like to thank the following for permission to reproduce photographs: Alamy pp. **11** (Robert Harding), **24** (The National Trust Photo Library), **9** (Photofusion picture library) **5, 7, 12, 16, 24, 25**; Corbis pp. **13** (Patrick Johns), **4, 19, 28b, 28d, 29b, 29d**; FLPA pp. **30** (David Hosking), **27**; Getty Images pp. **4, 5, 14, 17, 18, 19, 20, 22, 23, 26, 28a, 28c, 28e, 29a, 29c, 29e** (Photodisc); Holt Studios p. **8**.

Cover photograph of a Pasque flower (*Pulsatilla vulgaris*) reproduced with permission of NHPA/Laurie Campbell.

Our thanks to Patsy Dyer for her assistance in the preparation of this book.

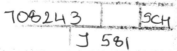
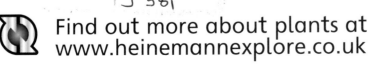

Find out more about plants at
www.heinemannexplore.co.uk

Contents

Words appearing in the text in bold,
like this, are explained in the Glossary.

What are plants?

Plants are living things. Like other living things they grow, feed and have young.

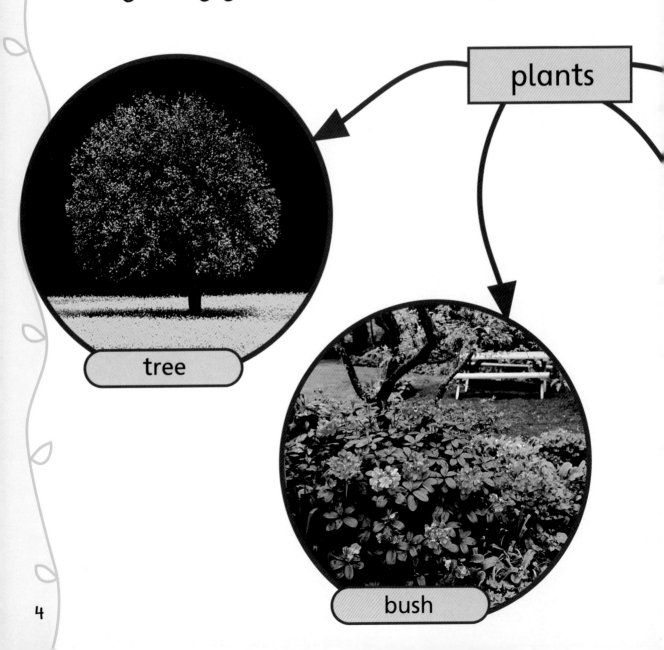

plants

tree

bush

There are many different kinds of plants in the world. They come in different sizes and shapes. **Weeds**, grass, trees, flowers, and bushes are all types of plants.

weeds and grass

flowers

Plant parts

Plants can look different but they are made up of the same parts. We group plants together because most of them have **stems**, leaves, flowers, **roots** and **fruit**.

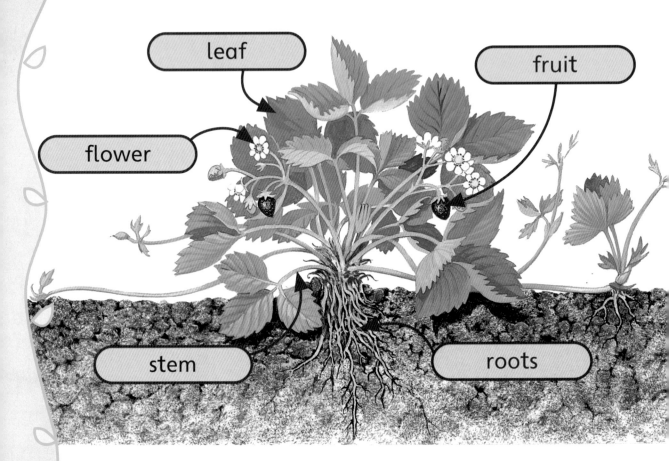

leaf

fruit

flower

stem

roots

What different parts can you see
on this plant?

What are roots?

Roots are the parts of the plant that grow under the ground. Different kinds of plants have different roots.

Plant roots are often white like these.

roots

Some plants have lots of small roots. Some plants have one big root.

Carrots are plant roots!

What do roots do?

Roots have two important jobs to do. Plants need water to grow. Root hairs on the root soak up water and **nutrients** from the soil.

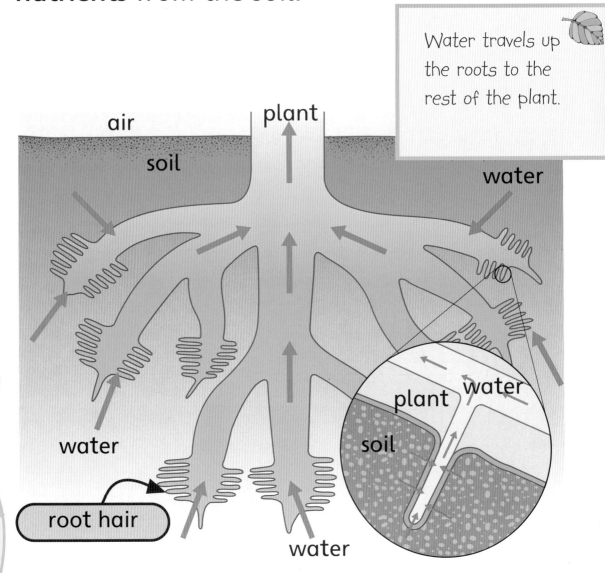

Water travels up the roots to the rest of the plant.

air

soil

plant

water

water

root hair

water

plant

soil

water

The other job that roots do is to stop the plant falling over. Roots hold the plant in the ground. Trees are heavy. They have big, strong roots to hold themselves up.

Strong roots stop this tree from being blown down by the wind.

What are stems?

Stems are plant parts that grow above the ground. They hold up the leaves and flowers.

stem

This plant has a tall, straight stem.

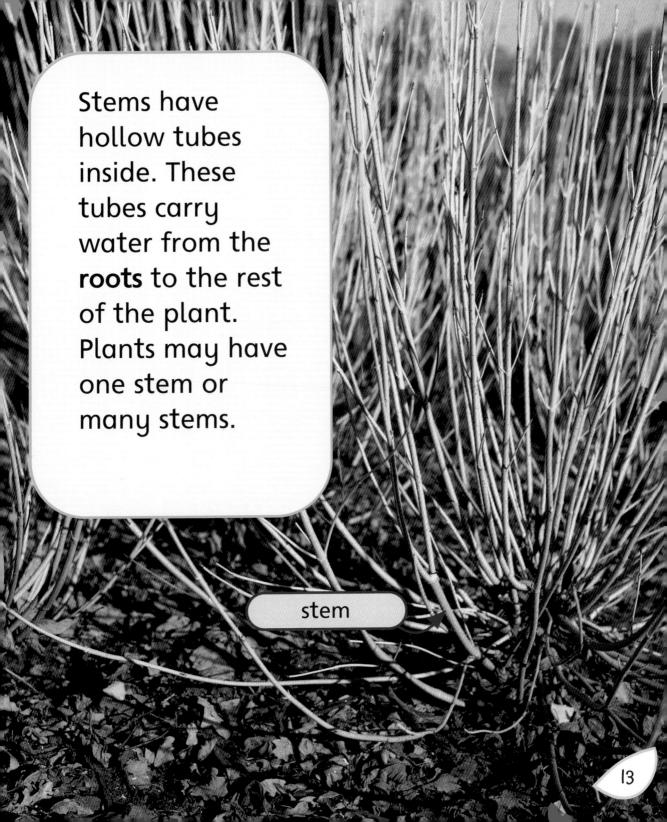

Stems have hollow tubes inside. These tubes carry water from the **roots** to the rest of the plant. Plants may have one stem or many stems.

stem

Kinds of stems

Tree **stems** are very thick, tall and strong. These special stems are called tree trunks.

The trunk of a tree is covered in a thick layer called bark.

bark

Some plants have thin stems.
These stems are not strong enough
to hold the plant up. So, the plant
climbs up other plants or sticks.

stem

This ivy stem climbs
up by growing
around a tree.

What are leaves?

Leaves make food for the plant. They use air, water and sunlight to make the food. **Stems** hold the leaves up so the sunlight reaches them.

Leaves on a plant are spread out so they are all in the light.

Water travels up to the leaves from the **roots** underground. Air moves in through little holes on the bottom of the leaf.

The lines on this leaf are like little hollow tubes. They bring water to the leaf.

Looking at leaves

There are many kinds of leaves. Some leaves are flat and wide. These leaves fall off their plants when it is winter.

oak

birch

Some plants, like pine and fir trees, have leaves all year round. That is why they are called evergreens. Their leaves are long and thin.

pine

sycamore

maple

What are flowers?

Flowers grow on **stems**. They start as a **bud** and open to show lots of colourful **petals**.

Flower petals can be yellow, pink, purple, red and even blue.

Can you *see* the seeds inside this sunflower?

Plants use flowers to make **seeds**. When seeds start to grow inside a flower, the petals die and fall off the plant.

Different flowers

Some plants have big flowers and some have small flowers. Some only have one flower and others have lots of flowers.

A tulip plant has one flower growing at the top of a single **stem**.

Some flowers grow at the top of a stem. Some flowers grow from the sides of a stem.

The flowers of a foxglove plant grow from the sides of the stem.

What are fruits?

Fruits are the parts of a plant that hold **seeds**. Seeds can grow into new plants. Some fruits are soft and juicy. Others are hard and dry.

The horse chestnut and the peach are both fruits because they both have seeds inside.

horse chestnut

peach

Fruits keep seeds safe while they grow. The fruit falls off the plant when the seeds have finished growing. Then the seeds can grow into new plants.

Tomato fruits start off green and turn red when the seeds inside are fully grown.

Odd ones out!

Some plants do not grow **fruits** and flowers like other plants. Conifer trees grow cones instead of flowers and fruit. Cones are wood-like and have scales.

Seeds grow between the cone's scales. Then the cone opens up and lets them fall.

scales

Ferns do not have fruits and flowers either. They make spores instead of seeds. Ferns and conifers are still plants because they make food in their leaves just like other plants.

The spores on these leaves can grow into new ferns.

spores

Try it yourself!

Fruit and other plant parts can be good to eat. They can help you grow. We should eat at least five different fruits and vegetables every day.

These are some plants that we eat. Do you know what they are?

These groups show which part of the plant these foods are. Can you think of some other plants that we eat that could go in these groups?

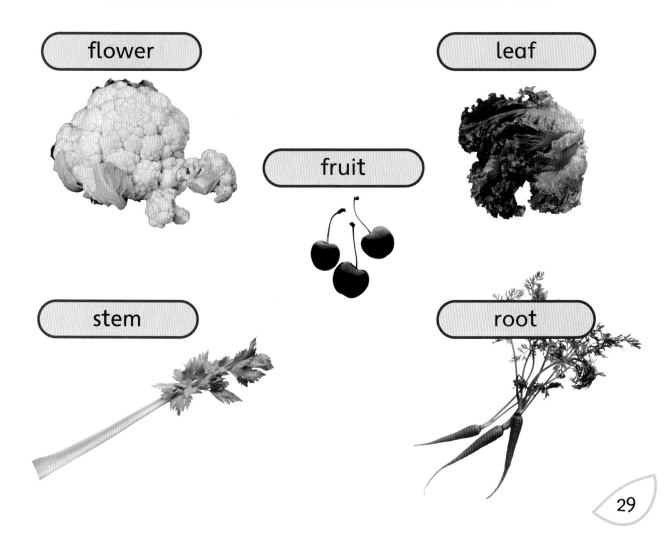

flower

leaf

fruit

stem

root

Amazing plants!

The raffia palm has longer leaves than any other plant. Its leaves grow up to 20 metres (65 feet) long. That is as long as two coaches!

 Find out more about plants at www.heinemannexplore.co.uk

Glossary

bud plant part that holds tiny leaves or flowers

energy living things need energy to grow and live

fruit part of a plant that holds its seeds

nutrient substance that living things need to grow

petal part of a flower

root plant part that grows underground and takes in water and nutrients from the soil

seed plant part that can grow into a new plant

stem part of a plant that leaves and flowers grow from

weed plant that people do not want or do not find useful

More books to read

Read and Learn: Life cycle of a broad bean, Louise Spilsbury (Raintree, 2004)

Read and Learn: Green foods, Isabel Thomas (Raintree, 2002)

Read and Learn: Leaves, Patricia Whitehouse (Raintree, 2004)

Index

Titles in the *World of Plants* series include:

WORLD OF PLANTS

How do plants grow?

Young Explorer

ANATOMY   GROWTH AND PROCESSES   HABITATS   REPRODUCTION

Hardback   0 431 01804 9

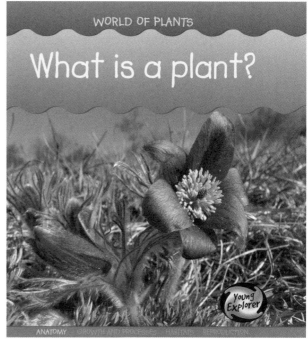

WORLD OF PLANTS

What is a plant?

Young Explorer

ANATOMY   GROWTH AND PROCESSES   HABITATS   REPRODUCTION

Hardback   0 431 01803 0

WORLD OF PLANTS

Where do plants grow?

Young Explorer

ANATOMY   GROWTH AND PROCESSES   HABITATS   REPRODUCTION

Hardback   0 431 01805 7

WORLD OF PLANTS

Why do plants have flowers?

Young Explorer

ANATOMY   GROWTH AND PROCESSES   HABITATS   REPRODUCTION

Hardback   0 431 01806 5

Find out about other titles from Heinemann Library on our website www.heinemann.co.uk/library